PORTFOLIO BUILDING

How to apply essential
concepts to real-world
situations ...

by Maria Crawford Scott

Editor, *AAII Journal*

AAII
AMERICAN
ASSOCIATION OF
INDIVIDUAL
INVESTORS®

"The American Association of Individual Investors is an independent, not-for-profit corporation formed in 1978 for the purpose of assisting individuals in becoming effective managers of their own assets through programs of education, information, and research."

For more information about membership, contact:

American Association of Individual Investors
625 N. Michigan Avenue
Chicago, Ill. 60611
(312) 280-0170, (800) 428-2244
www.aaii.com
ISBN: 1-88328-09-8

CONTENTS

Where Do You Begin?

"*Easier said than done*" is a common saying that applies well to developing an overall strategy for your investment portfolio. The basic concepts are relatively easy, but they become more complex and less clear-cut when it comes to applying them to real-world situations.

This book, *Portfolio Building Basics*, is designed to bridge the gap between theory and practice. In it, we'll take a look at specific individual circumstances, and see how portfolio strategies can be applied and implemented in practice.

DEALING WITH THE REAL WORLD

Developing a portfolio strategy starts with asset allocation, which consists of dividing up your portfolio among the major asset categories of stocks, bonds, and cash, and then among the major segments within those asset categories.

The asset allocation decision is extremely important—the decisions you make here will have a far greater impact on your overall portfolio return than more specific decisions, assuming you follow a well-diversified approach. These decisions are guided by risk and return considerations, and the tradeoff that exists between the two. But personal circumstances have a big effect on how each individual views risk and return. If these factors made no difference, everyone could follow the same portfolio. However, your tolerance for risk, your return needs (be it income or growth), the length of time you can remain invested, and your tax status all have an important impact on the kinds of investments you should be emphasizing and the kinds of investments you should avoid. Needless to say, major changes in your life will result in changes in your asset allocation strategy. Chapter 1 and 2 discuss how personal circumstances affect your asset allocation strategy.

To implement any strategy, you need to assess where you currently stand—what is included in your investment portfolio, and how is it currently allocated? An "investment portfolio" consists of all of your investible assets, including items that are sometimes overlooked, such as vested retirement plan assets and the cash build-up in cash value life insurance products. And real world investments don't always neatly fit into pre-defined categories. Chapters 3 and 4 focus on determining your current position.

Real world complexities also intrude in the transition stage. Transaction costs, taxes and limited retirement plan investment options make it more difficult for individuals to maneuver when

Putting Theory to Practice

Asset Allocation: Determining desired allocation among major asset classes (stocks, bonds, and cash) and then among those market segments based on your tolerance for risk, return needs, time horizon, and tax status.

Implementation: Determining where you currently stand, then gradually moving to desired allocation minimizing taxes and transaction costs. Or, if you have no current assets, starting a strategy from scratch.

Maintenance: Monitoring your individual investments and your overall portfolio for performance, and keeping it on track through periodic rebalancing.

shifting from one portfolio allocation to another. And younger individuals who are just starting out must deal with the complexities brought on by limited resources, such as investment minimums. Chapters 5 and 6 discuss implementing the transition stage of your portfolio.

Lastly, it is important to monitor your portfolio to make sure your asset allocation strategy remains on the course you originally intended. To gauge performance, using the right measure is critical; for investments without readily available performance statistics, you may have to do-it-yourself. And efficient approaches to portfolio rebalancing—making adjustments to your portfolio so that the original asset allocation percentages remain—will vary depending on whether you are still working or have entered retirement. The final chapters 7 through 11 examine portfolio tracking and fine-tuning.

The overall process of designing, implementing, and maintaining an effective asset allocation strategy is summarized in the figure above. The chapters of this book are structured around this process, and will provide you with the tools you need to navigate around life's complexities and steer you towards your investment goals.

1

Managing Your Portfolio: Making the Basic Asset Allocation Decision

The basic concepts behind many portfolio strategies are relatively easy in theory. But how do they work when applied to real-world situations?

In this booklet, Asset Allocation Workshop, we'll take a look at specific examples of individual circumstances, and see how the portfolio strategies can be applied in practice.

YOUR INVESTMENT FRAMEWORK: ASSET ALLOCATION

The first portfolio task faced by any individual is to set up an overall framework for the investment of your portfolio. This framework is built around your own personal investment profile, taking into consideration your return needs and your tolerance for risk. Another term for this is *asset allocation*, which consists of dividing your portfolio up among the major asset categories of stocks, bonds and cash.

Although asset allocation may seem simple—after all, you are only choosing among three categories—the decisions you make here will have a far greater impact on your overall portfolio return than any other more specific decision that you may make about your portfolio (assuming, however, that you follow basic investment principles in your other decisions, the most important of which is that you remain diversified among and within the various investment segments).

How does one set up an investment framework?

INVESTMENT PROFILES: AN EXAMPLE

Let's assume that you are in the early stages of retirement. Currently, your investment portfolio totals about $600,000 and you will need to withdraw about $25,000 each year from your investment portfolio to supplement annual income from your pension plan and Social Security. Let's also assume that you expect inflation to average around 4%.

The first step is to understand how the various aspects of your personal profile can affect your investment decisions. The most important considerations are: your tolerance for risk, your return needs, and your time horizon. Here's how your personal investment profile is likely to look:

Risk tolerance. The amount of risk you are willing to take on is important because if you take on

Table 1.
An Example of a Retiree's Investor Profile

Factors	Investor Profile	Additional Considerations
Risk Tolerance: How much of a loss can you stomach over a one-year period without abandoning your investment plan?	Moderate (6% to 15% loss)	Some downside risk must be tolerated to incorporate a growth component to protect against inflation.
Return Needs: What form of portfolio return do you need to emphasize: a steady sourceof income, growth, or a combination?	Combination: Some steady annual income, but also some growth	Don't rule out stocks entirely when considering income needs. Dividends provide income that grows. Also, growth investments can be used for income by investing for maximum total return, keeping a portion in cash for liquidity, and selling stock when necessary.
Time Horizon: How soon do you need to take the money out of your investment portfolio?	Combination of short-term (less than 5 years) for supplemental income and long-term (over 5 years) for growth and preservation of real value of portfolio	Cash and short-term bond investments are needed to provide liquidity for withdrawals each year.

too much risk, you could panic and abandon your plan; usually this occurs at the worst possible time.

The best measure of risk is to ask yourself how much of a loss you can stomach over a one-year period without bailing out of your investment plan. In general, investors with a low tolerance for risk can sustain losses of no more than 5% over a one-year time period; investors with a moderate risk tolerance can withstand total losses of between 6% to 15%; and investors with a high risk tolerance can withstand losses of between 16% to 25% annually.

Most individuals in their retirement years become somewhat less tolerant of risk because they are often relying on their portfolio for at least part of their annual income, and because they have less time to rebuild a portfolio should a significant loss occur.

However, even though your tolerance for risk may drop, it is important not to drop it entirely— some downside risk must be tolerated in order to incorporate a growth element into the portfolio to sustain its real value against the eroding effects of inflation. Higher growth, and therefore higher return, can only be achieved by taking on higher risk.

Return needs. This refers to the type of portfolio return you need to emphasize: A steady source of annual income, a high but variable growth potential, or a combination of the two. Determining your return needs is important because of the trade-off between income and growth: The price for a steady annual payment is lower growth potential.

Most retirees prefer a combination of growth and income. Some source of steady income is usually desired to assure that at least part of any needed income supplement is available. On the other hand, some growth is also needed to ensure that the value of your portfolio keeps pace with inflation; the minimum growth needed to do this would be the expected inflation rate. Thus, the need for a steady source of income needs to be balanced against the need to preserve the real purchasing power of your portfolio.

Although many retirees emphasize income investments, growth investments needn't be ruled out when considering income needs. Dividend income is usually lower than bond income at any given point in time, and dividends are also less assured than bond yields, but the long-term average is not unattractive, and that yield is a percentage on an increasing amount, since the underlying value of the stock will grow.

Also, it isn't necessary to rely on an income component if you need annual income. Growth investments can be used for income—you could, for instance, invest for maximum total return, keep a portion in cash for liquidity, and sell stock when necessary. While you may have to sell some stocks in a down market, dollar cost averaging (gradually selling off stocks over time) can help lower this timing risk, and the larger cash component supplies liquidity to help through the worst of a bear market.

This approach also has the advantage of reducing taxes, since you will be paying taxes only on capital gains (and possibly at a lower rate than income tax rates). Many mutual funds offer periodic withdrawal plans that allow this approach to be implemented relatively easily.

Time horizon. Your time horizon starts whenever your investment portfolio is implemented and ends when you will need to take money out of your investment portfolio. The time horizon is important because stocks are very volatile over short periods of time and are therefore inappropriate as short-term investments. In general, a short-term time horizon is less than five years and a longer-term time horizon is over five years.

For most retirees, the time horizon is a blend—partly short-term and partly longer-term.

The short-term horizon encompasses liquidity needs, which in this instance includes a $25,000 withdrawal each year (which nominally needs to be increased to preserve purchasing power) to supplement income. Cash provides a liquidity pool, and to the extent that resources are needed, this section of the portfolio should be increased to avoid any necessity to sell long-term investments unexpectedly.

Most retirees, though, expect to be living off of their funds for some time. For these needs, their investment horizon is longer-term.

PORTFOLIO COMBINATIONS

The next step is to examine various possible portfolio combinations to see how they might fit your personal investment profile. To do this, you should examine the risk and return potential characteristics of these combinations.

Table 2 presents risk and return characteristics for the three major asset categories. The figures are based on long-term annual averages for total return, annual capital growth and current yield, but it is important to keep in mind that these are long-term averages and significant year-to-year variations can be expected to occur. For downside risk, the figures are based on the worst loss over a one-year holding period during severe bear market conditions.

To help judge your tolerance for risk, use the downside risk figures as a guide to how much of a loss you can stomach. The average annual returns, broken down between growth and income, can be used to help assess your growth and income needs. Downside risk also serves as a guide to your time horizon, illustrating the risk involved with short-term time periods.

What do the figures show?

- Stocks contain the only real growth element, but this is achieved at high risk, with the possibility of a significant loss (--25%) during bear markets. Of course, this assumes that you are investing in well-diversified portfolio stocks that include growth stocks and the stocks of smaller firms.

- Bond investments, and to a lesser extent cash (money market funds), offer steadier sources of income, but no potential for growth.

- Cash investments, with no downside risk, offer liquidity and the ability to temper the overall downside risk of a portfolio. This component should be used for short-term investment horizons. On the other hand, the risk/return equation increasingly favors stocks over longer holding periods. In the table, the worst-case scenario for a one-year period is illustrated, but historically, the longer the holding period, the less likely you are to sustain a substantial loss in a stock portfolio. In other words, the worst-case scenario for stocks decreases for longer holding periods, and particularly for holding periods longer than five years.

The three major asset categories can be combined to produce any number of portfolios that can meet the needs of the investor profile outlined here. Table 3 presents the risk and return potential characteristics of three possible combinations.

How are these numbers derived?

The averages for each category in Table 2 are multiplied by the percentage allocated to each category, and then added together. For instance, the Conservative Portfolio consists of 50% in stocks, 40% in bonds, and 10% cash. The average annual return is:

$(50\% \times 11) + (40\% \times 7) + (10\% \times 4) = 8.7\%$

The downside risk for the combination portfolios assumes the worst-case scenario—that all three categories are down at the same time, a very conservative assumption that diversification has failed.

The table also shows the effects of inflation over time. The percentage of real growth indicates the amount to which the portfolio would grow after taking into account inflation; the dollar amount reflects the value to which the portfolio would grow stated in today's dollar terms. First-year income shows the dollar amount the portfolio would produce after the first year, while the real income after 10 years indicates the amount of income, in today's dollar terms, that the portfolio would produce. These figures make a number of assumptions that may be strained—for instance, it assumes that the portfolio is rebalanced to maintain the given percentage weightings in each category. However, it provides a rough illustration of the trade-offs that occur.

The conservative portfolio emphasizes bonds for a steady annual income—at 4.7%, it produces

Table 2.
Risk and Return Characteristics for Three Major Asset Categories

	Total Annual Return*	Average Annual Growth*	Average Annual Income*	Downside Risk**
Stocks	11%	8%	3%	-25%
Bonds	7%	0%	7%	-5%
Cash	4%	0%	4%	0%

* Based on long-term average estimates for total return, annual capital growth, and current yield; however significant year-to-year variation can be expected.
** An annual decline based on severe bear market conditions.

Table 3.
Risk and Return Characteristics for Combination Portfolios
(Based on a $600,000 portfolio and 4% inflation)

Retiree Portfolios (stocks/bonds/cash)	Total Annual Return (%)	Avg Annual Growth (%)	Avg Annual Income (%)	Downside Risk* (%)	Real Growth (after Inflation) in Portfolio Value		First-Year Income ($)	Real Value of Income in 10 Yrs. ($)
					(%)	Amt in 10 Yrs. ($)		
Conservative (50%/40%/10%)	8.7	4.0	4.7	-14.5	0.0	600,000	28,200	28,200
Moderate (60%/30%/10%)	9.1	4.8	4.3	-16.5	0.8	649,765	25,800	27,940
Aggressive (80%/0%/20%)	9.6	6.4	3.2	-20.0	2.4	760,590	19,200	24,339
Unsustainable** (20%/50%/30%)	6.9	1.6	5.3	-7.5	-2.4	470,597	31,800	24,942

* An annual decline based on severe bear market conditions. For the portfolios it assumes the worst-case assumption that diversification fails and all categories decline at the same time.

** Assuming 4% inflation, this portfolio will lose real value over time, reducing its purchasing power.

a little more than the $25,000 income required the first year. However, the 50% commitment to stocks provides a growth element of 4%—just keeping pace with inflation expectations. It also allows the income component to keep pace with inflation. The downside risk of −14.5% is the lowest of the three portfolios, close to the moderate range.

The second combination provides a more moderate mix that increases the stock component to 60%, decreases the bond component to 30%, and is 10% in cash. This provides an income that is close to the amount required—at 4.3%, it would produce about $25,800 after the first year. However, it provides at least a minimum of real growth in portfolio value, which also allows the income component to grow in real terms. The price is an increase in downside risk from the first combination.

The aggressive portfolio consists of 80% in stocks and 20% in cash. It does not supply a steady income—a 3.2% income level would provide only $19,200 after the first year, and the investor may have to use some of his growth portfolio to supplement income. On the other hand, the growth potential is quite large and more than makes up for the loss in steady income—at 6.4%, this provides a real (above inflation) growth of 2.4%, and allows the income component to grow as well. However, the price is an even steeper rise in downside risk—a loss of about 20% in the worst-case scenario. The 20% commitment to cash may seem high, but it tempers the downside risk. Alternatively, 10% could be shifted from cash to bonds to increase income, with a slight increase in downside risk.

The last portfolio is labeled "unsustainable," and is designed to show the problem with emphasizing steady income and a lack of tolerance for downside risk. It consists of only a 20% investment in stocks, 50% in bonds and 30% in cash.

In the worst-case scenario, this portfolio will sustain a loss of only 7.5%. However, the price is no growth—this portfolio will not keep pace with inflation, as you can see from the $470,597 value of the portfolio in real terms after 10 years. While it provides more than enough income the first year, the real value of this income is unable to keep pace with inflation.

POINTS TO REMEMBER

The sample portfolios here are simply examples—there are any number of combinations that are available to meet the various investment profiles of retirees. However, when you are examining the various combinations, keep these points in mind:

- A commitment of at least 50% in stocks will most likely be needed to provide growth and prevent the loss in real terms of the value of your portfolio. However, the stock portfolio must be adequately diversified and include growth stocks as well as some commitment to the stocks of smaller firms.

- Downside risk is a good way to judge risk tolerance, but keep in mind that some downside risk must be tolerated to allow a growth component in your portfolio.

- Growth investments can be used as sources of income, both from any dividends provided by stocks, and by simply selling stocks periodically to supplement income needs.

- Bonds provide income but no growth component. They also produce some downside risk. This downside risk can be reduced by keeping maturities on the shorter end (five to seven years) of the spectrum.

- Cash should be used to provide enough liquidity so that you are not forced to sell investments at inopportune times.

- Cash can also be used to moderate the downside risk introduced by a large stock component.

2

How Major Changes in Your Life Can Affect Your Asset Allocation

The asset allocation decision is a function of your risk tolerance, return needs (whether you need to emphasize current income or future growth), and your investment time horizon. When one of these conditions changes, it is time to reconsider your asset allocation.

When are changes likely to occur?

Individuals differ, and conditions may change simply because you have changed—for instance, you may tire of volatile changes in portfolio value and become more risk averse. Often, however, changes in these conditions coincide with major alterations in your life—in particular, retirement; asset allocation can be viewed as a function of your life cycle.

This chapter focuses on how major changes in your life can affect your asset allocation decision.

THE FACTORS AFFECTING ASSET ALLOCATION

Here's a rundown of the major conditions affecting asset allocation decisions, and how they may change over time.

Risk tolerance: Risk refers to the volatility of your portfolio's value. The amount of risk you are willing to take on is an extremely important factor because investors who take on too much risk usually panic when confronted with unexpected losses and abandon their investment plans midstream at the worst possible time. While some people do become more risk averse as they get older, risk tolerance is not necessarily a function of age; a conservative investor will go through changes in asset allocation over his life cycle, as will an aggressive investor.

Which investments are more volatile? Stocks are much more volatile than bonds and cash, and among stocks, the small stocks and international stocks are more volatile than large-cap stocks. However, stocks on average tend to produce higher total returns over the long term than do bonds or cash.

Return needs: This refers to whether you need to emphasize growth or income. Most younger investors who are accumulating savings will want returns that tend to emphasize growth and higher total returns, which primarily are provided by stocks. Retirees who depend on their investment portfolio for part of their annual income will want returns that emphasize relatively higher and consistent annual payouts, such as those from bonds and dividend-paying stocks. Of course, many individuals may want a blending of the two—some current income, but also some growth.

Investment time horizon: Your time horizon starts when your investment portfolio is implemented and ends when you will need to take the money out. The length of time you will be invested is important because it can directly affect your ability to reduce risk. Longer time horizons allow you to take on greater risks—with a greater total return potential—because some of that risk can be reduced by investing across different market environments. If your time horizon is short, you have greater liquidity needs—the ability to withdraw at any time with reasonable certainty of value. Volatile investments such as stocks lack liquidity and require a minimum five-year time horizon; shorter maturity bonds and money market funds are the most liquid.

Time horizons tend to vary over your life cycle. Younger investors who are only accumulating savings for retirement have long time horizons, and no real liquidity needs except for short-term emergencies. However, younger investors who are also saving for a specific event, such as the purchase of a house or a child's education, may have greater liquidity needs. Similarly, investors who are planning to retire, and those who are in retirement and living off of their investment income, have greater liquidity needs.

Changes Over Your Life Cycle

Table 1 presents two examples of how major changes in your life may affect your asset allocation. The table shows the changing allocations for two individuals over their lifetime: one a more conservative investor, and the other a more aggressive investor.

These two investors, of course, start at different points—the conservative investor with a 70% commitment to equities, primarily in the more conservative large-cap sector; the aggressive

Table 1.
How Major Changes Can Affect Your Asset Allocation

| Asset Category | Conservative | | | Aggressive | | |
	Early Career (%)	Late Career (%)	Retirement (%)	Early Career (%)	Late Career (%)	Retirement (%)
Cash	10	10	10	10	10	10
Bonds	20	30	40	0	10	10
Large-Cap Stocks	40	40	40	30	40	50
Small-Cap Stocks	15	10	5	30	20	15
International Stocks	15	10	5	30	20	15

investor with a 90% commitment to equities, evenly split among the large-cap, small-cap and international segments. Their responses to major changes over their life cycle reflected by their asset allocations, however, are similar.

To begin with, both investors have at least a 10% commitment to cash at all points in their life cycle, reflecting the need of all investors for some liquidity for short-term emergencies. In addition, both investors in Table 1 have at least a 50% commitment to equities at all points in their life cycle, reflecting the need of most investors for some exposure to growth.

Some individuals may view a 50% commitment to stocks as being not particularly conservative for a retiree; the allocations here are not recommendations, but simply examples. Keep in mind, however, that even retirees need to protect their future income from declines in purchasing power due to inflation. The trade-off for greater income is lower total returns; an overemphasis on current income can cause serious erosion in the real value of the portfolio down the road, resulting, ironically, in an actual decrease in the real value of the income that the portfolio is providing.

Over time, as their income and liquidity needs increase, both investors increase their commitments to bonds and cash, the aggressive investor moving from 10% to 20%, while the conservative investor moves from 30% to 50%. In addition, both investors decrease their commitments to the more volatile segments of the equity markets—small-cap stocks and international—for more stability and for greater emphasis on the dividend-paying portion of the stock market.

However, both investors keep at least a small portion of their portfolios committed to the small-cap stock and international stock market segments for diversification in the equity markets. A stock portfolio that excluded these segments as being "too risky" and only invested in large-cap stocks would actually be more risky.

Of course, other life changes could cause an investor to move from one stage to another. For instance, a married couple with no children and who consider themselves aggressive investors may have a child and turn more risk averse, or a retiree may win the $40 million lottery and not have to worry any longer about living off of retirement savings.

In addition, changes in your life may not necessarily cause a change in the conditions affecting your asset allocation decision. For instance, an investor with a large portfolio may not need to increase current income during retirement, and his asset allocation may remain the same as that in his early career stage.

Your own asset allocation life cycle will very likely be different than the examples presented here. While the changes in your life that affect the asset allocation decision won't be frequent, it is important to reassess your allocation when they occur.

3

Defining Your Investment Portfolio

Before you can begin to implement any asset allocation strategy, you first must take stock of where you currently stand. What does your current investment portfolio look like? And to assess that, you need to understand the definition of an investment portfolio. In other words: What does an investment portfolio consist of?

The Concept of an Investment Portfolio

Why does it matter what you include in your investment portfolio? The primary reason to take stock of your investment portfolio is to determine an appropriate asset allocation, in particular among the three major asset categories—equities, fixed income, and cash.

When you make an asset allocation decision, you should match the investment characteristics of the various asset categories to your own personal return goals and risk preferences in a manner that will maximize return and minimize risk. If you misdefine your investment portfolio, you may wind up with an asset allocation that is less efficient in meeting your needs.

An investment portfolio should consist of financial assets that you would be willing to sell for spending money or that generate some form of spending money, either now or some time in the future. Many items are obvious—for example, your personal investments such as mutual funds, stocks, and bonds. But other items are less clear. For instance, what about your house or the income you receive from your pension plan?

Here are some questions to ask yourself when trying to determine whether uncertain items should be included:

1) Is there a dollar value that you can attach to it? Some assets are difficult to value—for instance, stock options on your employer's stock. If the value is vague, its inclusion in your overall portfolio will add little meaning, and would serve only to confuse your allocation strategy.

2) Is it of substantial or material value? Some items may not be worth much relative to your other assets—for example, you may only carry small balances in your checking account. If the item is not worth much relative to your other assets, it is not worth the effort to add it to your overall portfolio.

Table 1.
Defining Your Portfolio

Assets You Should Include in Your Investment Portfolio

Personal Investments, Including:
Checking accounts—Valuation: Current market value; Asset class: Cash
Certificates of deposit—Valuation: Current market value; Asset class: Fixed income
Money market funds—Valuation: Current market value; Asset class: Cash
Credit union accounts—Valuation: Current market value; Asset class: Fixed income
Mutual funds—Valuation: Current market value; Asset class: Varies
All securities—Valuation: Current market value; Asset class: Varies
U.S. savings bonds—Valuation: Current market value; Asset class: Fixed income

Trusts:
For child's education—Valuation: Current market value; Asset class: Varies
Named income beneficiary—Valuation: Present value of income; Asset class: Fixed inc.
Named principal beneficiary—Valuation: Current market value; Asset class: Varies

Insurance-Related Products:
Cash value life—Valuation: Current surrender value less term; Asset class: Fixed income
Annuities, accumulation stage—Valuation: Current surrender value; Asset class: Varies
Annuities, payout stage—Valuation: Current contract value; Asset class: Varies

Investment Real Estate—Valuation: Estimated current market value; Asset class: Varies

Tax-Deferred Investments & Retirement Plans:
IRAs, SEPs, and Keoghs—Valuation: Current market value; Asset class: Varies
Defined contribution plans such as 401(k)s, 403(b)s, and profit-sharing plans—Valuation: Current market value; Asset class: Varies
Defined Benefit Plans—Valuation: Present value of current payments; Asset class: Fixed income

Social Security—Valuation: Present value of payments; Asset class: Fixed income

Assets You Shouldn't Include in Your Investment Portfolio:

- Your home
- Collectibles
- Uncertain or distant inheritances
- Uncertain or distant pension and Social Security benefits
- Personal possessions such as: furniture, art, boats and autos, personal jewelry

3) Is it an asset that, if not included in your portfolio, would cause you to structure your portfolio differently? An example could be pension payments you are receiving after retirement—excluding these payments from consideration may cause you to invest a substantially higher amount in fixed-income securities than would otherwise be the case; they should therefore be included.

4) Is it an investment asset or a consumption asset? An investment asset is a financial asset that you would not mind liquidating for cash to spend and should be included in your investment portfolio. A consumption asset is purchased for purposes other than simply investment, such as your home (a housing need) or a collectible (a hobby or desire); these would be more difficult to part with and should not be included in your investment portfolio.

WHAT COUNTS?

When you include assets in your investment portfolio, two questions will arise:

- How should they be valued? Assets in your investment portfolio should be valued at their current market value, but you may have to make estimates or rough calculations for certain items that are not readily marketable or whose current value is unclear.

- What major asset category should they be included in? Equities, fixed income, and cash are the three major asset categories, but some assets don't easily fit into one of these categories.

Here's a rundown, summarized in Table 1, of what you should include in your investment portfolio, with special attention to uncertain items and how they can be valued and categorized.

- **Personal investments:** Most of these items are relatively straightforward—stocks, bonds, mutual funds, etc. Items you may overlook include certificates of deposit, U.S. savings bonds and credit union accounts. What about your checking account? If you use it as a place to hold substantial amounts of cash, it should be considered part of your liquid investments, which counts as cash.

- **Trusts:** If you have set up a trust in which you have deposited money to pay for your child's education, this should be considered part of your overall investment portfolio. The trust approach is used to save taxes, but in the absence of the trust, you would still have to set aside personal investments to pay for this expense.

  If you are a named beneficiary of a trust, and the amount is substantial, you should probably include this in your investment portfolio, since the inclusion or exclusion of this could affect your overall asset allocation decision. If you are a named beneficiary of the principal, you should use the current market value of the assets and categorize them as they are currently invested. If you are a beneficiary of the income from the trust, the stream of payments should be treated as if it were a fixed-income payment, although in actual fact it may vary somewhat. The current value of this income stream can be estimated by the approach illustrated in Table 2. The estimated amount would then be included in your investment portfolio as, in effect, a fixed-income investment.

- **Insurance-related products:** Cash value life insurance includes a savings component that should be included in your overall investment portfolio. However, it also includes an insurance component that is not an investment. The value to include in your investment portfolio can be estimated by taking the current surrender value and subtracting the premium you would need to pay for term insurance with equivalent coverage. Since the investment portion grows at a fixed rate, this should be treated as a fixed-income investment in your investment portfolio.

  Fixed and variable annuities, in their accumulation stages when you are paying into them, are primarily tax-deferred investment products (although there is a small insurance portion) and they should therefore be included in your investment portfolio. These can be valued at their current surrender value. Fixed annuities should be treated as fixed-income investments. However, variable annuities allow greater investment choices, and the asset category depends on how you have chosen to invest in the subaccounts.

  Annuities in their payout stages provide an income stream that may be fixed or variable, lasting for various time periods—it all depends on the payout option you have chosen. These should be included in your investment portfolio, with a value equal to the contract value in your most recent statement. The asset category depends on how you have chosen to have the underlying assets invested; if in a fixed-interest account, it should be treated as fixed income; if in a variable account, the categories would vary based on your choices.

- **Investment real estate:** Real estate that you have purchased purely for investment purposes should be included in your investment portfolio. While REITs (real estate investment trusts) are easily valued, you will have to use estimated current market values for direct purchases and limited partnerships. Which asset category should they fall under? The best approach is to examine the type of returns that will be generated—if primarily income (as in rental property and mortgage REITs), you may want to place it in the fixed-income category; if mostly appreciation (equity REITs), treat it as an equity.

- **Tax-deferred investments:** All of your tax-deferred investments, including those you have set up on your own and those sponsored by your employer, should be considered part of your investment portfolio.

  Tax-deferred investments you may set up yourself include IRAs, as well SEPs, and Keoghs (for the self-employed).

Table 2.
Estimating the Present Value of a Stream of Payments

To estimate the present value of a stream of future periodic payments, multiply the current annual payment by the present value annuity factor in the table. The annuity factor chosen should be the one that corresponds with:

- The expected number of years the payments will last—for instance, if the payments are to last for your life, use your current life expectancy, and
- An expected interest rate

No. of Years	4%	5%	6%	7%	8%	9%	10%
5	4.45	4.33	4.21	4.10	3.99	3.89	3.79
10	8.11	7.72	7.36	7.02	6.71	6.42	6.14
15	11.12	10.38	9.71	9.11	8.56	8.06	7.61
20	13.59	12.46	11.47	10.59	9.82	9.13	8.51
25	15.62	14.09	12.78	11.65	10.67	9.82	9.08
30	17.29	15.37	13.76	12.41	11.26	10.27	9.43
35	18.66	16.37	14.50	12.95	11.65	10.57	9.64
40	19.79	17.16	15.05	13.33	11.92	10.76	9.78

equal to the current rate paid by a Treasury bond with a maturity equal to the number of years the payments will last. As an example, let's assume that you are currently receiving pension payments that total about $6,000 annually. If your life expectancy is 25 years and the rate paid on a 25-year Treasury bond is roughly 7%, the corresponding annuity factor is 11.65. Multiplying your $6,000 annual payment by the 11.65 annuity factor produces an estimated present value of $69,900. This $69,900 should be included in your investment portfolio and treated as if it were a fixed-income asset when making asset allocation decisions.

Employer-sponsored defined contribution plans include 401(k)s, 403(b)s, and profit-sharing plans. You should include all of your own contributions and the vested portion of any employer contributions as part of your investment portfolio.

Employer-sponsored defined-benefit pension plans are more complicated: These retirement plans provide an income stream based on your salary and years with your employer. Including pension payments that you are currently receiving in your portfolio could substantially change the way you would allocate any investments that you do control. How should you value a pension you are currently receiving? The current value of this income stream can be estimated using the approach illustrated in Table 2. This value should then be treated in your investment portfolio as a fixed-income asset.

- **Social Security payments:** The rationale for including these payments in your portfolio if you are currently receiving them is the same as with defined-benefit pension plans. The value can be estimated in the same way, and it should be treated as fixed income.

What Doesn't Count?

Which assets don't meet the four-question test and therefore shouldn't be included in your investment portfolio?

- Your house: Assets that are used for consumption should not be included in your investment portfolio. Most families do not purchase homes strictly for investment purposes. Usually, if you sell a home, you must buy another one to live in. If you intend to "downsize" at some point, wait until you receive the sale proceeds, and then reassess and rebalance your portfolio. The same reasoning applies to vacation homes.

- Collectibles: Usually these are simply hobbies and are really more consumption assets. In addition, they are hard to value, they are illiquid, and you would be unlikely to sell them to meet future needs.

- Uncertain or distant inheritances: Uncertainty makes the valuation process—and thus the allocation decision—too murky, and therefore meaningless.

- Uncertain or distant pension and Social Security benefits: Again, uncertainty of full vesting (and Social Security's future) makes the valuation process too murky and meaningless.

- Personal possessions: These are consumption items and typically of insubstantial value (taken individually) relative to your total portfolio.

If you have an item that is not listed in the "what counts" or "what doesn't count" list, try to answer the four questions raised initially to see if it meets the inclusion test.

Above all, be realistic and conservative and try to keep the process from becoming overly complex. Don't spend a lot of time worrying about every minor detail, or valuing an asset down to the last dollar—asset allocation is important, but it does not depend on pinpoint accuracy.

4

How to Calculate
Your Asset Allocation

Once you have defined your investment portfolio, you can measure where you stand currently. How do you calculate your current asset allocation?

DETERMINING WHERE YOU STAND: AN EXAMPLE

The process is relatively straightforward, although as we shall see, certain investments can cause complications.

Table 1 illustrates the process using a sample portfolio of investments that includes both mutual funds and individual stocks. (The examples were selected for illustration purposes only).

The table provides a listing of all of the investor's holdings. It includes the investor's entire portfolio—all taxable savings, such as mutual funds, individual stock holdings and money market funds, as well as tax-deferred savings, including retirement plan assets, to which the investor is fully entitled (for instance, here it includes all vested assets in an employer-sponsored profit-sharing plan).

The table categorizes these holdings, first according to their major asset category, and then further breaking them down into the market segment of the asset category into which they fall. The percentage of the holding that is committed to these categories is also indicated. In this list, only one holding—the Dodge & Cox Balanced Fund—has an objective that commits itself to more than one category at a time.

The current market value of each holding is also listed, and is totaled at the bottom of the list. Dividing the market value of each holding by the market value of the total portfolio indicates the percentage of the total portfolio represented by that holding.

The last column consists of special considerations to note when assessing your current asset allocation.

Table 2 shows how allocations are calculated. For each holding, the percentage of the holding that is committed to the category (in most instances, 100%, or 1.0 in decimal form) is multiplied by the percentage it represents of the total portfolio; the percentages are then added together for each category.

The first series allocates the holdings among the three major asset categories. The result? This investor's portfolio has 56.5% committed to stocks, 18.5% committed to bonds, and 25% committed to cash—a relatively conservative asset mix.

The second series breaks the holdings down further, allocating them among the market segments. The result: This investor's portfolio has 34.5% committed to U.S. large-cap stocks, 15% committed to small-cap stocks, and 7% invested in foreign stocks; 18.5% committed to domestic bonds; and the remaining 25%, of course, in cash.

Table 1.
Determining Your Current Asset Allocation: An Example

Current Holdings	Major Asset Category	Segment of Asset Category	Market Value of Holdings ($)	(As % of Portfolio)	Special Considerations
Mutual Funds (Category)					
Dodge & Cox Balanced (Balanced)	60% stock, 40% bond	60% large-cap stock, 40% domestic bond	30,000	15%	Allocation changes not dramatic
Strong Total Return (Growth & Income)	100% stock	100% large-cap stock	17,000	8.5%	Market timer
Acorn (Growth)	100% stock	100% small-cap stock	18,000	9%	25% in foreign stock as of 12/31/94
Scudder Capital Grth (Growth)	100% stock	100% large-cap stock	15,000	7.5%	Maintains commitment to stocks
Harbor Bond (General Bond)	100% bond	100% domestic bond	25,000	12.5%	11% in cash as of 10/31/94
Vanguard Trustees' Int'l (International)	100% stock	100% foreign stock	14,000	7%	Broad-based int'l diversification
Individual Stocks					
Profit-Sharing (Co. Stock)	100% stock	100% large-cap stock	13,000	6.5%	Individual stock
Microsoft	100% stock	100% large-cap stock	3,000	1.5%	Individual stock
AT&T	100% stock	100% large-cap stock	3,000	1.5%	Individual stock
Zoom Telephonics	100% stock	100% small-cap stock	5,000	2.5%	Individual stock
American Filtrona	100% stock	100% small-cap stock	3,000	1.5%	Individual stock
Canandaigua Wine	100% stock	100% small-cap stock	4,000	2%	Individual stock
Cash					
Money Market Fund	100% cash		50,000	25%	
Total			**200,000**	**100%**	

Table 2.
Determining Your Asset Allocation: An Example

Determining Allocation Among Major Asset Categories

Amount in stocks:
$(0.60 \times 15\%) + (1.0 \times 8.5\%) + (1.0 \times 9\%) + (1.0 \times 7.5\%) + (1.0 \times 7\%) + (1.0 \times 6.5\%) + (1.0 \times 1.5\%) + (1.0 \times 1.5\%) + (1.0 \times 2.5\%) + (1.0 \times 1.5\%) + (1.0 \times 2\%) = 56.5\%$

Amount in bonds:
$(0.40 \times 15\%) + (1.0 \times 12.5\%) = 18.5\%$

Amount in cash:
$(1.0 \times 25\%) = 25\%$

Determining Allocation Within Segments of Asset Categories

Amount in U.S. large-cap stocks:
$(0.60 \times 15\%) + (1.0 \times 8.5\%) + (1.0 \times 7.5\%) + (1.0 \times 6.5\%) + (1.0 \times 1.5\%) + (1.0 \times 1.5\%) = 34.5\%$

Amount in U.S. small-cap stocks:
$(1.0 \times 9\%) + (1.0 \times 2.5\%) + (1.0 \times 1.5\%) + (1.0 \times 2\%) = 15\%$

Amount in foreign stocks:
$(1.0 \times 7\%) = 7\%$

Amount in domestic bonds:
$(0.40 \times 15\%) + (1.0 \times 12.5\%) = 18.5\%$

Amount in individual stocks:
$(1.0 \times 6.5\%) + (1.0 \times 1.5\%) + (1.0 \times 1.5\%) + (1.0 \times 2.5\%) + (1.0 \times 1.5\%) + (1.0 \times 2\%) = 15.5\%$

This second series could also be broken down by the portion of the stock and bond portfolios that are committed to their market segments. For instance, of the total stock portfolio, 61.1% (34.5% divided by 56.5%) is committed to U.S. large-cap stocks, 26.5% (15% divided by 56.5%) is in U.S. small caps, and 12.4% (7% divided by 56.5%) is in foreign stocks. Similarly, 100% of the bond portfolio is committed to domestic bonds.

POSSIBLE PROBLEMS: CATEGORIZATION

Determining the major asset categories, and the market segments of your own holdings may not be as straightforward as it appears at first glance.

For instance, a balanced mutual fund, such as the Dodge & Cox Balanced fund, invests in both stocks and bonds; it would therefore fall into both the stock and bond asset categories in proportions that are roughly representative of the fund's holdings. Pinpoint precision is unnecessary and misleading, since a fund's holdings are continuously changing. For funds that have relatively steady allocations, the investment objective outlined in the fund's prospectus should provide you with an allocation guideline.

Funds that vary their holdings by large amounts—for instance, those that try to time the market—are much more difficult to categorize. For instance, the Strong Total Return Fund's objectives allow it to move from a position that is fully invested in stocks to one that is fully invested in bonds or cash. In recent years it has maintained a fairly high commitment to stocks; however, its cash position recently has varied from 19% to only 7% over a six-month period.

Funds that vary their allocations take away some of the control you have over your personal asset allocation strategy. What should you use in determining your own allocation? Examine the prospectus to see where the fund's objectives commit it most of the time; if it is uncertain, use history as a guide—for instance, look at its positions as stated in the last four quarterly reports or last two semiannual reports. AAII's *Individual Investor's Guide to Low-Load Mutual Funds* also provides asset category breakdowns for the funds it covers. Since the Strong Total Return Fund has primarily been committed to stocks, it is classified as 100% in the stock category here.

For similar reasons, the Harbor Bond Fund is classified here as 100% in the bond category. This fund does not have as much latitude as the Strong Total Return Fund, but its cash commitment varied recently from as high as 20% to 11%, just a little higher than the typical mutual fund, which can be expected to hold a small cash position for shareholder redemptions.

The Acorn Fund presents another interesting dilemma. This fund is usually categorized as a small-cap fund, and it is, except that it has expanded its small-stock universe overseas. For several years, Acorn has had as much as 25% of its assets invested in foreign small-cap stocks. Acorn has a relatively low portfolio turnover, and its foreign commitment has been relatively stable for several years. Should its market segments be broken down between foreign and U.S. small caps? In the table here, we have not, but an argument certainly could be made for it. In that case, the holding would represent a 6.75% ($0.75 \times 9\%$) commitment to small-cap stocks and a 2.25% ($0.25 \times 9\%$) commitment to foreign stocks. And that would raise the total foreign stock commitment to 9.25%.

Lastly, individual stock holdings should, of course, be included and categorized according to the market segment into which they fall: The last three individual stocks in the table, with market capitalizations (number of shares outstanding times share price) of under $500 million, are smaller capitalization firms; an ADR of a foreign firm, of course, would fall within the foreign stock segment.

WHERE YOU CURRENTLY STAND

Once you have determined where you stand, you should assess your current portfolio in light of your move toward your desired asset allocation, with the ultimate goal of being fully diversified.

For instance, our sample investor has a 7% holding in foreign stocks, which consists of an investment in the Vanguard Trustee's Equity International fund, a broadly diversified foreign fund. If this foreign stock commitment, however, consisted of a single ADR holding, further diversification in this segment would be warranted.

For that reason, the very last item in the table totes up the individual stock holdings. In general, a total of 10 unrelated stocks is the bare minimum to assure adequate diversification within a stock portfolio. This investor has only six stocks, but they do not make up his entire stock portfolio. Instead, they represent 15.5% of the total portfolio, or 27% of the portion committed to stocks (15.5% divided by 56.5%); the remaining stock holdings are in well-diversified mutual funds. On the other hand, this investor should consider adding new individual stock holdings, or committing more to diversified stock funds, rather than investing further in the individual stocks he already owns.

Before you can figure out how to get to where you want to go, you need to know where you stand. Determining your current asset allocation is not complicated, and will enable you to get to your ultimate destination—your desired asset allocation.

5

Handling the Transition When Implementing a Strategy

Once you have developed an asset allocation strategy, you should stick to it. However, there are times when there will be changes in your investor profile that may necessitate an overhaul of your strategy. Or, you may currently hold a hodgepodge of investments and have decided that you need to develop and implement a strategy. Whatever the reason, changing asset allocation strategies means that you will be making major changes to your portfolio. How do you make the transition?

THE TRANSITION: AN EXAMPLE

Table 1 presents a transition phase that you may want to consider. It is based on the example used in the previous chapter, which discussed how to determine your current asset allocation. The investor in this example started investing with no real strategy in mind, and ended up with the assortment of investments in Table 1, including a balanced fund that is 60% in stocks and 40% in bonds, and six individual stock holdings, three of which are small companies. When he determined his asset allocation, he discovered he held 56.5% in stocks (34.5% in large-cap stocks, 15% in small-cap stocks, and 7% in foreign stocks), 18.5% in bonds, and 25% in cash.

After examining his current allocation, this investor now realizes that, based on his own circumstances and risk tolerance, he is undercommitted to stocks. His ideal mix, he has decided, is very aggressive—an 80% commitment to stocks (45% of the portfolio in large-cap stocks, 20% in small caps, and 15% in foreign stocks), 10% in bonds, and 10% in cash.

How should he make the transition?

First, he must determine which funds or stocks to emphasize or add, and which to de-emphasize.

Does it make sense to add new mutual funds to reach his goal? If there are no funds that he currently owns that will help him meet his new allocation goals—if, for instance, he wanted to add foreign stocks and didn't currently own a foreign fund—it would make sense to add a new fund to his holdings. Or, if there is a different fund that he prefers to an existing fund, he may want to add that fund. However, there is no reason to "diversify" among funds of similar type. The portfolio itself is diversified. Adding funds that are in similar categories can be counterproductive, creating a closet index fund—in other words, the combination of similar funds performing like an index fund, yet at the higher cost of active management, reflected in higher expense ratios.

What about adding more stocks to his portfolio of individual stocks? Currently, he only holds six stocks, not enough to be diversified in a stand-alone portfolio, but this investor's mutual fund holdings do offer a counterweight. However, given the level of holdings in the stocks he already owns, he probably would not want to add shares to those stocks—if he does anything with his individual holdings, it would be better to add new stocks, rather than add to his existing holdings.

In this example, we'll assume that our investor is happy with his existing funds and stocks, and will work within his current holdings.

Given his desired asset allocation, this investor needs to add funds to all three stock categories—large caps, small caps, and foreign. Of course, over time there will be differing changes in value of the various funds due to market movements, but for this illustration we'll make the simplified assumption of no change.

To meet his large-cap target, committing more funds to the balanced fund would make no sense, since that would also add to his bond commitment. And it would make little sense to add to the Strong Total Return, a fund that tends to time the market, which means that at any given time, those funds may or may not be committed to stocks. Thus, the investor decides to add to Scudder Capital Growth for his large-cap portion.

How much? His desired allocation to large-cap stocks is 45%, and his unchanged large-cap holdings aside from Scudder Capital Growth total 27% (8.5% in Strong Total Return, 9% in Dodge and Cox Balanced, and 9.5% in individual stocks); that implies an 18% commitment (45% − 27%) to Scudder, or $36,000 (18% of $200,000). To reach that level, he must add $21,000.

For the additional commitment to small-cap stocks, the selection is easy, since he is happy with Acorn (which is closed to new investors, but not to existing shareholders). His desired allocation is 20%, and he has 6.0% in individual small-cap stock holdings, which implies a 14% commitment to Acorn—an addition of $10,000 to reach a total of $28,000 (14% of $200,000).

Similarly, he is happy with Vanguard Trustees' International for foreign stocks. His desired allocation is 15%, or $30,000, and to reach it, he must add $16,000.

De-emphasizing bonds means a withdrawal from the Harbor Bond fund. Since his investment in Dodge & Cox Balanced fund already gives him a 6% commitment to bonds, he must reduce his Harbor Bond fund holdings to 4%, or $8,000—a withdrawal of $17,000.

Lastly, reducing his cash commitment to 10% of his portfolio means a hefty withdrawal from the money market fund of $30,000.

TIMING

When should all of this be accomplished?

Many individual investors recognize that it is risky to try to time the market, moving into or out of the market based on a "prediction" of the opportune moment. An asset allocation strategy is a buy-and-hold approach designed to keep you invested across all market environments, a form of time diversification.

The same principle holds true when making changes in a portfolio. It is impossible to predict with accuracy when the best time is to invest in any of these investment categories, and attempting to do so can easily backfire, resulting in an investment at the worst possible time. Moving large amounts of money from stocks to bonds, or the reverse, should be done gradually, in roughly equal payments over a two-year period, to reduce the impact of the market at one point in time.

Table 1.
Changing Your Asset Allocation Strategy: The Transition

Current Allocation:

34.5% Large-Cap Stocks		
15.0% Small-Cap Stocks		
7.0% Foreign Stocks		
56.5% Stocks	18.5% Bonds	25% Cash

Desired Allocation:

45% Large-Cap Stocks		
20% Small-Cap Stocks		
15% Foreign Stocks		
80% Stocks	10% Bonds	10% Cash

Holding	Asset Class	Current Allocation ($)	Current Allocation (%)	Desired Allocation ($)	Desired Allocation (%)	Change ($)	Quarterly Change ($)
Scudder Capital Growth	Large Cap	15,000	7.5	36,000	18.0	+21,000	+2,625
Strong Total Return	Large Cap	17,000	8.5	17,000	8.5	0	0
Dodge & Cox Balanced	Large Cap/Bonds	30,000	15.0	30,000	15.0	0	0
Acorn	Small Cap	18,000	9.0	28,000	14.0	+10,000	+1,250
Vanguard Trustees' Int'l	Foreign	14,000	7.0	30,000	15.0	+16,000	+2,000
Individual Stocks (Large Cap)	Large Cap	19,000	9.5	19,000	9.5	0	0
Individual Stocks (Small Cap)	Small Cap	12,000	6.0	12,000	6.0	0	0
Money Market Fund	Cash	50,000	25.0	20,000	10.0	-30,000	-3,750
Harbor Bond	U.S. Bonds	25,000	12.5	8,000	4.0	-17,000	-2,125
	Total	**200,000**		**200,000**			

Table 2.
Targets Assuming a Growing Portfolio Over 2 Years

	Allocation (%)	Allocation ($)
Scudder Capital Growth	18.0	45,900
Strong Total Return	8.5	21,675
Dodge & Cox Balanced	15.0	38,250
Acorn	14.0	35,700
Vanguard Trustees' International	15.0	38,250
Individual Stocks (Large Cap)	9.5	24,225
Individual Stocks (Small Cap)	6.0	15,300
Money Market Fund	10.0	25,500
Harbor Bond Fund	4.0	10,200
		Total: $255,000

How frequent should the moves occur? Markets can change dramatically over the course of a year, and for that reason yearly changes are too infrequent. Monthly is an alternative, although for some it may be overly cumbersome, particularly for sales, which may result in complex tax computations. Quarterly changes are probably the easiest to accomplish, spreading the transition over various market environments without being overly burdensome.

Table 1 illustrates a quarterly transition over a two-year period. The total changes over that period are divided into eight equal installments, which represent equal quarterly changes over the next two years.

THE TAXING PROBLEM

Adding to existing funds or new funds poses no real costs to this investor (assuming you are using no-load funds). Similarly, the withdrawal from the money market fund involves no costs.

The withdrawal from the bond fund, however, could result in potentially costly tax liabilities. If you have a choice and, to reach your allocation target, can switch among holdings in a tax-sheltered environment (a 401(k) plan, IRA or other retirement plan, for instance), try to use those funds to accomplish the change. You may also be able to offset taxes on gains with losses elsewhere, although this may interfere with the quarterly changes outlined above—it is a balancing act, and you will have to decide.

If you are retired and living off of your retirement assets, simply withdraw from the targeted investments.

In addition, you may want to consider the addition of new money generated from salary, income and capital gains distributions, or one-time sources such as an inheritance. Make sure you are reinvesting distributions from existing funds to the new targets, and, obviously do not reinvest in those you want to de-emphasize.

If you take growth into consideration, you will find that you needn't withdraw as much from categories you are de-emphasizing than in a static scenario. For instance, assume that you are able to add $15,000 to your portfolio each year, and that in addition, your total portfolio will grow by about 6% over the next two years. That means that, at the end of two years, your portfolio will grow to over $255,000. A 4% commitment to Harbor Bond fund would be $10,200, a decrease of $14,800 (or, $1,850 each quarter), rather than the $17,000 implied in the static portfolio.

Assuming a growing portfolio, of course, would alter all of the investment commitments (see Table 2); you could use these target amounts when directing the investment of new money.

Even the growth scenario, however, assumes equal growth in all investments—an unlikely event. Don't worry about pinpoint accuracy when moving to a new asset allocation strategy. Your portfolio mix will be constantly changing with the markets and you should monitor it periodically (quarterly or semiannually). Use new money to fine-tune your portfolio rather than selling taxable assets in order to reach an accurate asset allocation mix. Substitute concerns for minimizing transaction costs and taxes for asset mix precision, and don't worry about straying from your targets by several percentage points.

6

How to Implement a Strategy If You Are Starting From Scratch

Imagine this scenario:

You are young and you just received a $2,000 bonus check—your first entry into your investment/savings program.

To begin your investment program, you go through the whole asset allocation process—first determining your allocation among the major asset categories and then further down among the major stock market segments. And you come up with this mix: cash, 10%; intermediate-term bonds, 10%; and stocks, 80%—with the latter split 80% in a "core" holding of large-capitalization stocks (which would be 64% of your total portfolio), 10% in the stocks of smaller firms, and 10% in foreign stocks (8% of your total portfolio in each).

With much enthusiasm, you then sit down to implement your strategy by divvying up your savings: $200 to a money market fund, $200 to an intermediate-term bond fund, $1,280 to a large-cap fund and $160 each to a small-stock and an international fund. Then you select several mutual funds that match your goals.

Unfortunately, that's as far as you get in implementing your plan—because each fund has a minimum initial investment of $2,000.

Not all funds, of course, have a $2,000 initial minimum. Some are lower, but many—and particularly the large fund families—are the same or higher. While you could search the mutual fund universe for funds with low minimums, it is not a good idea to base fund selection primarily on the required minimum initial investment.

How, then, can you start an effective investment program from scratch? Here are some approaches that can help you build toward your goal.

COUNTING ALL SAVINGS

First, make sure that you are including all forms of savings when you are considering how much you have to invest and how it is to be allocated. In particular, make sure that you take into consideration the fully vested portion of any employer-sponsored savings plans, such as 401(k)s, and any IRAs.

Most mutual funds have lower minimum initial investment for IRAs. And many 401(k) plans offer several investment options with no minimums. By investing these assets in the lowest percentage allocation in your asset allocation plan, you can more easily meet the minimum initial requirements with your taxable savings.

For instance, let's continue with the scenario outlined at the beginning, but let's also assume that you have $2,000 in a 401(k) plan with a number of investment options. Your total investment portfolio is actually $4,000, which would be allocated: $400 each to a money market fund and intermediate-term bonds; $320 each to international and small-cap stocks, and $2,560 to core equities. Your $2,000 in taxable savings would meet the minimum initial investment for your "core" stock fund; the smaller commitments would be made within your 401(k) plan.

What if your 401(k) plan options are more limited? Consider first meeting your allocation among the major asset categories: cash, bonds, and stocks, with your stock portion 100% invested in your "core" large-cap stock holdings. You can then build toward your other allocations, as outlined below.

STARTING FROM ABSOLUTE SCRATCH

If you are literally starting from scratch—you have no other forms of savings—the process is more difficult. While you should have your ultimate allocation goal in mind, the fact of the matter is that when you are starting from scratch, you will not be able to implement your full investment program at once. Instead, you will have to build toward it.

How can that be done?

First, you should make sure that you have enough savings to meet your liquidity needs—you do not want to be in the position of being forced to withdraw funds from your investment program to meet emergencies or other cash needs. Once you have established a cash reserve, you can start to build your plan.

Here are two approaches.

A *Balanced* Start: Under this approach, you would start your investment program by investing in a balanced or asset allocation fund that divides its assets in a relatively set range between stocks, bonds, and cash. Additional investments can be made to the fund until you have saved enough to begin investing in funds in more specific market segments.

The disadvantage, however, is that you cannot control the allocation—and many younger investors seek heavier commitments to stocks than is typical of balanced funds.

Another disadvantage is that as you build up your savings, you will most likely outgrow the balanced fund—in other words, you will want to switch from the balanced fund to several different funds according to your asset allocation plan. If your balanced fund consists of taxable savings, you will have to pay taxes on any gains when you switch.

If you use this approach, make sure that you fully understand your chosen fund's investment approach because the names can be confusing. Some funds that call themselves "asset allocation funds" try to time the various market segments by changing their asset mix depending on their outlook. These types of funds should be avoided.

Other funds that call themselves "asset allocation" funds have a relatively fixed allocation to the major market segments; funds that refer to themselves as "balanced" also tend to have fixed allocations. These are the funds you should stick with, since they will ensure exposure to the three major market segments at all times. However, check to be sure that the fund you have selected is committed to the major market segments in which you want to be invested.

Concentrating on Core Stocks: This is the strong stomach approach: You save up to the minimum initial investment of a broad-based stock index fund, and then invest the entire amount in it.

The disadvantage, of course, is that you are fully exposed to the stock market. But since you are just starting out, you most likely have a very long-term time frame (possibly over 30 years) and can afford to take on substantial stock market risk.

The index fund serves as the core of your overall portfolio as you start to build toward your investment plan. It will be the most conservative portion of your stock market commitment, composed primarily of large-capitalization stocks; when you add on, you will be adding on more aggressive commitments—small stocks and international, for instance.

Starting with a core and building around it minimizes the tax consequences for taxable savings—instead of selling fund shares that no longer meet your needs and upon which you may have taxable gains, you are simply buying and holding, and adding.

Using an index fund gives you exposure to the stock market, but takes out "manager risk"—the risk that the active investment decisions made by a portfolio manager will cause the fund to deviate substantially from the overall market. For investment newcomers, this makes the mutual fund selection less daunting.

However, you do need to focus on an appropriate index. Since the fund will be your core stock holdings, you should select one that targets a large-cap stock market index, such as the Standard & Poor's 500 or a broader index that still encompasses large-cap stocks, such as the Wilshire 5000. In addition, you should make sure that the fund you select adequately follows the targeted index.

If you are going to use this approach, you first need to reconsider your risk tolerance and see if you can stomach starting out with a full commitment to stocks using a broad-based index fund. You also need to make sure that you will not need any portion of this investment for liquidity needs.

DIVERSIFYING BEYOND THE CORE

Once you have picked a starter fund, whether it be a balanced fund or index fund, keep adding to it over time and gradually build up your commitment. Concentrate first on meeting your allocation goals among the three major market segments—cash, bonds, and core stocks.

If you started with a balanced fund, you may want to next add a stock fund (once you can meet the minimum) to increase your percentage investment in stocks, and perhaps an intermediate-term bond fund after that; you can then start the switch out of the balanced fund.

If you started with a core index fund, you could next add the minimum to an intermediate-term bond fund (in fact, you will have created your own "balanced" fund).

At what point do you start diversifying beyond the major market segments—in particular, when should you consider diversifying your stock portfolio beyond the core?

The answer will be a function of:

• The minimum initial investments of the funds that you have chosen, and

• The percentages that you plan to commit to the other market segments. Keep in mind that to have a meaningful effect, you really need a minimum commitment of around 10% to any market segment.

For instance, let's assume the mutual funds you are eyeing have a $2,000 minimum initial investment. If your goal is 10% each to international and small stocks, you should start adding other funds once your stock portfolio has reached $20,000; if you added those funds earlier, you would have a greater commitment to those segments than planned.

If you are a more aggressive investor—for instance, you will be committing only 50% of your stock portfolio to the "core" market portfolio, and you want to divide the remainder of your portfolio to small stocks and international (25% each), you could start adding these funds sooner— you could start when you have accumulated as little as $8,000 in your stock portfolio.

Which segment should you add first? Pick the one to which you will be committing the larger percentage. What if you plan equal commitments? You could choose either one, so pick the fund that you are more comfortable with or one that has other attractions (for instance, perhaps lower minimums).

Start-Up Tips

If you are starting an investment program from scratch, keep these points in mind:

- First build up and maintain a cash reserve to meet short-term emergencies and other liquidity needs.

- Try to develop an overall investment strategy that you are aiming for, even if you can't implement the strategy immediately.

- Select mutual funds that meet your investment strategy first; use the minimum initial investment as a secondary consideration.

- Select a balanced fund (for less aggressive investors) or a broad-based index fund (for more aggressive investors) for your initial investment, and build from there.

- The minimum initial investment of the funds that you have selected will set the investment savings goal that you are trying to achieve.

- The percentage commitment to each stock market segment will determine when you should start adding funds to your initial investments.

- Don't agonize over small deviations from your overall allocation plan. For instance, if a minimum investment in a small stock fund results in a 12% or 13% commitment to small stocks, rather than 10%, go ahead and make the commitment. Your overall allocation goal is only a rough guide.

7

Monitoring Your Portfolio: Measuring the Performance of Your Components

Most investors "watch" their portfolio intently. But there are better ways to do it than others.

What is the best way to watch your portfolio to make sure it will meet your financial goals?

Primarily, it consists of monitoring it to make sure it is living up to expectations, and making the necessary changes when it isn't.

Monitoring your portfolio involves performance measurement, and there are two types of portfolio measurement that need to be performed. First, there is your overall portfolio. Measuring the performance of your total portfolio is useful to see if the long-term terminal value that you hoped to achieve with your investment program is realistic. This does not have to be done frequently (yearly or every few years is sufficient) and will be covered in the next chapter.

The second type of performance measurement, and the topic of this chapter, concerns the various parts of your portfolio. This performance monitoring and measuring should be done much more frequently, either quarterly or semiannually. The purpose is to see how well the professional expertise you have hired or are performing yourself is doing. For instance, you should examine the performance of each mutual fund against its peers (funds with similar objectives) and an appropriate index (one that covers investments similar to those in the fund) over the same time period. These peer-group returns and indexes provide benchmarks that allow you to judge the manager's performance.

MONITORING MUTUAL FUND PERFORMANCE

For mutual fund holdings, it isn't necessary to make your own calculations to measure the performance; in fact, it is difficult to do it yourself with much accuracy. Instead, use one of the many publications that provide information on mutual fund performance, including AAII's *Individual Investor's Guide to Low-Load Mutual Funds*; most publications also provide appropriate benchmarks for comparison.

Some individuals prefer to calculate their own performance because they want to see how the fund is doing for them. For instance, if you have recently purchased or sold shares and you paid a load, this can be taken into consideration if you calculate your own performance. However, your self-calculated returns will not answer the question: How well has the fund manager performed? The answer to this question determines whether you should remain with the fund or consider moving elsewhere. For this, it is easier to stick with the outside sources.

Monitoring Your Stock-Picking Ability

If you are investing in stocks on your own, measuring your individual stock portfolio performance against an appropriate index or similarly managed mutual fund can provide you with an idea of your own investment decision-making ability. The purpose is to determine how well your stock selection strategy is doing. You may not want to fire yourself, but if your performance is not up to par, you may want to revise your selection strategy.

The simple approach presented here will give you an approximation of your own stock portfolio return. Although the resulting answer will not be precise, the return approximation will be close enough for an individual to make informed decisions. (If you have a computer, investment software is available that can perform precise calculations.)

Most of the information you will need to calculate your return is contained in the typical brokerage account statement. Your total return consists of the change in value of your investment, plus any income provided by the investment during the investment period. In the typical brokerage account, dividends and interest payments are swept into (reinvested in) an interest-bearing cash account or money market fund, so the ending balance of a typical statement reflects both the market value of the securities and income from those investments. The only adjustment that needs to be made concerns any cash additions to or withdrawals from the account. (If you use several brokerage firms, simply consolidate the information contained on the various statements for the same time periods.)

Figure 1 presents a brokerage statement covering one quarter (three months). The first section, Account Transaction Detail, describes all transactions that occurred over this time period. All dividends were reinvested in the money market fund. In addition, two stocks were sold, and the proceeds were used to buy two stocks. Additional funds were also needed, however, to pay for the stock purchases, and so money was added to the account (indicated by "funds received"). Funds were also withdrawn from the portfolio (indicated by "funds withdrawn"). Lastly, transaction costs (1%) were deducted when incurred, and are therefore reflected in the total market value (the "amount" column) of each security.

The second portion of the statement provides the Portfolio Position Detail as of the end of the period. Figure 1 also provides the portfolio position at the beginning of the period (as of January 1) so you can see more clearly how the portfolio in this example changed.

Table 1 summarizes the portfolio positions over the period, and provides the return calculation.

Figure 1.
Brokerage Account Summary (January 1 Through March 31)

ACCOUNT TRANSACTION DETAIL

DATE	TRANSACTION	QUANTITY	DESCRIPTION	AMOUNT
			Opening Cash Balance	$0.00
01-03	Dividend Received		Federal Screw Works	$10.00
01-03	Bought	10	Money Market Fund	($10.00)
01-03	Dividend Received		Money Market Fund	$3.66
01-03	Reinvestment	3.66	Money Market Fund	($3.66)
01-06	Dividend Received		Oilgear Co.	$10.00
01-06	Bought	10	Money Market Fund	($10.00)
01-25	Dividend Received		Trans-Lux Corp	$9.45
01-25	Bought	9.45	Money Market Fund	($9.45)
02-01	Dividend Received		Salem Corp	$21.00
02-01	Dividend Received		Tranzonic Cos. Cl A	$9.00
02-01	Bought	30	Money Market Fund	($30.00)
02-01	Dividend Received		Money Market Fund	$3.68
02-01	Reinvestment	3.68	Money Market Fund	($3.68)
02-22	Dividend Received		Noland Co.	$6.60
02-22	Bought	6.6	Money Market Fund	($6.60)
02-27	Sold	200	Money Market Fund	$200.00
02-27	Funds Withdrawn		Funds Withdrawn	($200.00)
03-01	Dividend Received		Method Electrs Inc. Cl B Conv	$3.00
03-01	Dividend Received		Seaway Food Town Inc.	$20.00
03-01	Dividend Received		Watsco Inc Cl B	$6.50
03-01	Bought	29.5	Money Market Fund	($29.50)
03-01	Dividend Received		Money Market Fund	$3.70
03-01	Reinvestment	3.7	Money Market Fund	($3.70)
03-17	Funds Received		Funds Received	$2,000.00
03-20	Bought	2000	Money Market Fund	($2,000.00)
03-24	Sold	300	Motts Hldgs Inc @ 4.25	$1,262.25
03-24	Sold	400	Nycor Inc Com New @ 2.75	$1,089.00
03-24	Sold	2660.62	Money Market Fund	$2,660.62
03-24	Bought	300	Allegheny & Western @ 11.25	($3,341.25)
03-24	Bought	300	TCI Intl Inc @ 5.625	($1,670.62)
03-31			Closing Cash Balance	$0.00

PORTFOLIO POSITION DETAIL

QUANTITY	SECURITY DESCRIPTION	MARKET VALUE ON MARCH 31		MARKET VALUE ON JANUARY 1	
		SHARE PRICE	TOTAL	SHARE PRICE	TOTAL
STOCKS					
300	Allegheny & Western	$11.750	$3,525.00	Bought 3/24	$0.00
100	Federal Screw Works	$19.250	$1,925.00	$19.625	$1,962.50
100	Methode Electrs Inc. Cl B Conv	$18.000	$1,800.00	$17.000	$1,700.00
100	Noland Co.	$21.125	$2,112.50	$19.375	$1,937.50
100	Oilgear Co.	$16.000	$1,600.00	$13.750	$1,375.00
200	Salem Corp	$24.375	$4,875.00	$19.125	$3,825.00
200	Seaway Food Town Inc.	$14.500	$2,900.00	$11.125	$2,225.00
300	TCI Intl	$5.500	$1,650.00	Bought 3/24	$0.00
300	Trans-Lux Corp	$8.625	$2,587.50	$9.125	$2,737.50
200	Tranzonic Cos. Cl A	$15.250	$3,050.00	$15.750	$3,150.00
100	Watsco Inc Cl B	$18.250	$1,825.00	$15.938	$1,593.80
300	Motts Hldgs Inc	Sold 3/24	$0.00	$4.313	$1,293.90
400	Nycor Inc Com	Sold 3/24	$0.00	$2.938	$1,175.20
MONEY FUNDS					
	Money Market Fund	$1.000	$117.51		$871.54
	Net Portfolio Value		$27,967.51		$23,846.94

Table 1.
Calculating Return

Summary of Portfolio Positions:

Portfolio Beginning Value:	$23,846.94
Net Additions*:	$1,800.00
Portfolio Ending Value:	$27,967.51

Approximate Return Equation:

$$\left[\frac{\text{Ending Value} \ - \ 0.50 \ (\text{Net Additions*})}{\text{Beginning Value} + 0.50 \ (\text{Net Additions*})} - 1.00 \right] \times 100 = \text{Return (\%)}$$

Use net withdrawals, a negative number, if total withdrawals are greater than total additions.

Example:

$$\left[\frac{\$27,967.51 \ - \ 0.50 \ (\$1,800)}{\$23,846.94 + 0.50 \ (\$1,800)} - 1.00 \right] \times 100 = 9.4\%$$

CALCULATING THE RETURN

The return calculation compares ending values to beginning values, and adjusts for the impact of net additions or withdrawals from the portfolio. This adjustment is made by decreasing the ending value and increasing the beginning value by 50% of the net additions or withdrawals.

In the example here, the portfolio was valued at $23,846.94 at the beginning of the period (the ending value of the prior statement), and it was valued at $27,967.51 at the end of the period. During this time, $2,000 was added to the account, and $200 was withdrawn, for a net addition of $1,800; 50% of $1,800 is $900, so the adjusted ending value is $27,067.51, and the adjusted beginning value is $24,746.94.

Dividing the adjusted ending value by the adjusted beginning value indicates the change in value for the period; in this example the ending value is 1.094 times the beginning value. Subtracting 1.00 eliminates the beginning value, so the answer is in the form of an increase in value—the return—which in this example is a gain of 0.094, or 9.4% for the quarter.

If the ending value after adjusting for net withdrawals or additions is less than the beginning value, the division will produce a figure that is less than 1.00 [for example 0.80]; subtracting 1.00

Figure 2.
Worksheet for Calculating Your Return

Total Ending Value:
Use the ending value of your brokerage statement.

_____ **Line 1**

Net Additions or Withdrawals:
Add up all monies added to the portfolio, and subtract all monies withdrawn from the portfolio. The resulting figure is your net additions (a positive number) or net withdrawals (a negative number, if withdrawals were greater than additions).
Multiply this figure by 0.50.

_____ Net additions (or withdrawals)

× 0.50 = _____ **Line 2**

Adjusted Ending Value:
Subtract Line 2 from Line 1 to determine Adjusted Ending Value. Note that if Line 2 is negative, subtracting a negative number is the same as adding a positive number.

_____ Line 1

- _____ Line 2

= _____ **Line 3**

Total Beginning Value:
Use the beginning value of your brokerage statement (the ending value of the prior statement).

_____ **Line 4**

Adjusted Beginning Value:
Add Line 2 to Line 4 to determine Adjusted Beginning Value. Note that if Line 2 is negative, adding a negative number is the same as subtracting a positive number.

_____ Line 4

+ _____ Line 2

= _____ **Line 5**

Percentage Return:
Divide Line 3 by Line 5

_____ Line 3

÷ _____ Line 5

= _____ **Line 6**

Subtract 1.00 from Line 6

- 1.00 = _____ **Line 7**

Multiply Line 7 by 100

× 100 = _____ % Return

then produces a negative figure [0.80 − 1.00 = −0.20, or −20%], and the return represents a loss.

How does this return of 9.4% for this portfolio compare with similar portfolios? This portfolio consists primarily of smaller company stocks selected at random from a larger portfolio for illustration purposes only. The return is close to the overall market during this time (the S&P 500 was up 9.7% for the same quarter), but somewhat higher than the small-stock Russell 2000 index, which was up 4.6%, and higher than the 6.8% for aggressive growth funds over the same quarter.

ADJUSTING FOR SPECIAL SITUATIONS

What if your brokerage account statement includes mutual funds that you do not want to include in the calculation?

Adjust the beginning and ending account statement values by subtracting the market value of those funds based on prices at the beginning and ending dates; also subtract from the ending value any distributions from those funds that are swept into the brokerage firm's money market fund or cash account.

What if you do not use a brokerage account, but instead hold your own stock certificates? Determine the market value of your stocks at the beginning and ending of the period measured, and add any dividends received to the ending value. Then adjust for any additional investments or withdrawals as in the example here.

SIMPLE ARITHMETIC

Monitoring the components of your portfolio is important to determine if changes need to be made. If you use the approximation formula for individual stock holdings, it is not as complicated as you may think. Figure 2 is a worksheet for determining your own stock portfolio return.

8

Are You on Track? Measuring Your Portfolio's Performance

The question of every investor is: How'm I doing? Although a few are satisfied simply watching the dollars grow, most investors want that translated into a performance figure.

And with good reason. Measuring the performance of your total portfolio is useful to see if the long-term terminal value that you hope to achieve with your investment program is realistic.

In general, you should be examining the return on your portfolio to make sure it is within the target range you expected, based on the investment mix you have settled upon. If it isn't, you may need to make some adjustments in your future projections—for instance, you may have to increase your savings rate, you may have to take on more risk to achieve the target that you set, or you may simply have to adjust your target value downward, settling for less in the future.

Method 1: The Sum of the Parts

There are two ways you can calculate the return of your portfolio.

The first method is a sum of the individual parts: the return for each holding is multiplied by the percentage of the total portfolio that the holding represented at the beginning of the period; these "weighted" returns are then added together for the total portfolio return.

The information needed for this calculation method is relatively easy to obtain; if you are monitoring the individual holdings in your portfolio (as you should be), this information should be right at your fingertips.

The market values for your holdings at the beginning and ending of the period are on mutual fund and brokerage account statements. For the returns of mutual fund holdings, you can use one of the many publications that provide information on mutual fund performance, including AAII's annual *Individual Investor's Guide to Low-Load Mutual Funds*. If you are investing in stocks on your own, the approximation method provided in the last chapter [and repeated in the box on page 48] can be used for your own stock portfolio return. Of course, if you have a computer, investment software is available that can perform precise calculations.

Table 1 illustrates the calculation. The first part of the table presents a listing of this investor's total portfolio holdings during the first quarter of 1995. The market value of each holding at the start and end of the period is indicated, along with the percentage of the total portfolio that each holding represents.

The quarterly return column indicates the first quarter return for each portfolio. For the mutual fund holdings, the information is based on returns reported by AAII's *Quarterly Low-Load Mutual Fund Update* for the indicated period. For the individual stock portfolio, the return was calculated using the approximation method.

The equation labeled Return Calculation #1 shows how the portfolio return was determined, using the portfolio percentages at the beginning of the quarter, and the quarterly returns. This method provided a quarterly portfolio return of 4.5%.

METHOD 2: THE END VS. THE BEGINNING

The second method uses the same approximation equation that was used to determine the stock portfolio's return [see box labeled Approximate Return Equation on page 48]. This calculation compares the total market value of all holdings at the end of the period to the total market value of all holdings at the beginning, and adjusts for the impact of net additions or withdrawals to the overall portfolio. The adjustment is made by decreasing the ending value and increasing the beginning value by 50% of the net additions or withdrawals.

In the example here, there were several withdrawals and additions to individual holdings—for instance, $1,800 was taken from the money market fund to invest in individual stocks. However, the overall portfolio had a net withdrawal of $4,000, as this investor apparently decided to use some savings for consumption.

The portfolio was valued at $167,926.00 at the beginning of the period, and it was valued at $171,460.73 at the end of the period. Since $4,000 was withdrawn from the portfolio, the adjusted ending value is $173,460.73 [$171,460.73 − (50% × −$4,000); note that subtracting a negative figure is the same as adding a positive number]; the adjusted beginning value is $165,926.00 [$167,926.00 + (50% × −4,000); note that adding a negative figure is the same as subtracting a positive figure].

Dividing the adjusted ending value by the adjusted beginning value indicates the change in value for the period; in this example the ending value is 1.045 times the beginning value. Subtracting 1.00 eliminates the beginning value, so the answer is in the form of an increase in value— the return—which in this example is a gain of 0.045, or 4.5% for the quarter. The result is the same as the return determined by the first method. Of course, the resulting answers using the approximation method will not always be precise, but it will be close enough for an individual to make informed decisions.

If the ending value after adjusting for net withdrawals or additions is less than the beginning

Table 1.
Measuring Portfolio Performance

Current Holdings	Beginning Period (1/1/95) Market Value of Holdings ($)	(%)	Quarterly Return (%)	Net Additions (Withdrawals) ($)	Ending Period (3/31/95) Market Value of Holdings ($)	(%)
Dodge & Cox Balanced (Balanced: 60%/40%)	30,236.97	18	7.8	(4,000.00)	28,439.45	17
Strong Total Return (Growth & Income)	17,437.94	10	6.6		18,588.84	11
Acorn (Small Cap)	18,396.73	11	2.7		18,893.44	11
Scudder Capital Growth (Growth)	15,387.69	9	3.4		15,910.87	9
Vanguard Trustees' Int'l (International)	14,976.92	9	0.1		14,991.90	9
Individual stock portfolio (Small Cap)	23,846.94	14	9.4*	1,800.00	27,967.51	16
Harbor Bond (General Bond)	25,968.03	16	4.1		27,032.72	16
Bull & Bear Gold Investors	5,578.93	3	-10.0		5,021.04	3
Money Market Fund	16,095.85	10	2.1	(1,800.00)	14,614.96	8
Total	167,926.00	100		(4,000.00)	171,460.73	100

Return Calculation #1

(18% x 7.8) + (10% x 6.6) + (11% x 2.7) + (9% x 3.4) + (9% x 0.1) + (14% x 9.4) + (16% x 4.1) + (3% x -10.0) + (10% x 2.1) = 4.5%

Return Calculation #2:

$$\left[\frac{171,460.73 \quad - 0.50(-4,000)}{167,926.00 + 0.50(-4,000)} - 1.00 \right] \times 100 = 4.5 \%$$

Weighted Index Returns:[†]

(29.8% x 9.7) + (25% x 4.6) + (9% x 1.9) + (23.2% x 5.7) + (3% x -2.2) + (10% x 1.2) = 5.6%

[†]Based on reported quarterly returns of:

S&P 500	9.7%
Russell 2000	4.6%
MS EAFE Index	1.9%
Salomon Corp. Bond Index	5.7%
Average Gold Fund	-2.2%
Treasury Bills	1.2%

*Return calculation for stock portfolio:

$$\left[\frac{\$27,967.51 - 0.50\ (\$1,800)}{\$23,846.94 + 0.50\ (\$1,800)} - 1.00 \right] \times 100 = 9.4\%$$

value, the division will produce a figure that is less than 1.00 (for example 0.80); subtracting 1.00 then produces a negative figure [0.80 − 1.00 = −0.20, or −20%], and the return represents a loss.

WEIGHTED INDEXES

Measuring the performance of your total portfolio helps you assess the accuracy of the long-term return assumptions you made when determining your asset allocation mix.

While you can compare your portfolio's actual performance to your assumptions, you should also compare the assumptions and your portfolio performance to an index. Of course, indexes exist for asset classes, not entire portfolios, so you need to "create" your own index. You can do this following the method used in the first return calculation. First, determine the percentage of your portfolio that is allocated to each asset class, and multiply the percentage by the total return for the appropriate index (be sure the return reflects price changes and any income generated); the sum of these weighted returns is an appropriate index that you can use to judge your portfolio's actual return.

For example, this investor has 29.8% of his portfolio in growth and income stocks (60% of the Dodge & Cox Balanced holding, which is both stocks and bonds, plus Strong Total Return and Scudder Capital Growth); 25% in small stocks (Acorn and the individual stock portfolio); 9% in international (Vanguard Trustee's International); 23.2% in bonds (40% of Dodge & Cox Balanced plus Harbor Bond), 3% in gold (Bull & Bear Gold Investors) and 10% in money market funds.

The last part of Table 1 lists the appropriate indexes for these asset categories (the average return for gold mutual funds was used), and their same-quarter returns. The equation labeled Weighted Index Returns shows how the portfolio index was calculated, producing a weighted index return of 5.6%, which is above the 4.5% return for this investor's portfolio. The difference may prompt this investor to re-examine some of his individual holdings to see if they are performing adequately.

You should also compare this weighted index return with the long-term return assumptions you used when you determined your asset allocation mix. If they are close, but your own portfolio returns are off, the individual holdings should be reviewed. On the other hand, if your long-term assumptions are different than the weighted index return, you may want to rethink your original assumptions.

A Long-Term Outlook

Taking stock of your total portfolio is necessary to make sure that you will meet your long-term goal. How often should this be done?

While the example here used quarterly returns, portfolio measurement does not need to be done frequently. Once a year is sufficient for most individuals.

If you do measure your portfolio's performance more frequently—for instance, quarterly—you can determine the annual return by adding 1.00 to each quarterly return figure (in decimal form), multiplying the four numbers, and subtracting 1.00 from the final figure. The result is the annual return in decimal form. For instance, if the returns in the prior three quarters for the investor in Table 1 were 3%, 1.2%, and 0.2%, his annual return (through March 31, 1995) would be: $[1.03 \times 1.012 \times 1.002 \times 1.045] - 1.00 = 0.091$, or 9.1%.

However, if you measure portfolio performance frequently, don't make hasty decisions based on short-term results. Use the short-term results to satisfy your curiosity and as a possible warning signal. But keep in mind that you are assessing a long-term strategy.

9

Portfolio Tuning and Maintenance During Your Working Years

Most vehicles require tuning and maintenance, and that goes for investment vehicles, as well.

Tuning consists of making sure your portfolio is allocated in the most tax-efficient manner, so that the greatest amount of the return possible goes to you, rather than Uncle Sam.

Maintenance consists of rebalancing your portfolio, to make sure that variations in performance of the individual items do not cause your overall asset allocation to stray too far from your original plan.

All investors, regardless of age, need to tune and maintain their portfolios. However, the methods available to you to keep it in balance may differ, depending on whether you are still in your working years and continuing to save, or if you are in your retirement years, withdrawing money from savings upon which to live.

This chapter will focus on the working years and the next chapter will focus on retirement.

Tuning for Tax Efficiency

Your portfolio consists of all of your savings, including those that are put into a retirement account such as an IRA or an employer-sponsored retirement plan such as a 401(k).

Why include retirement assets in your portfolio?

In our current tax structure, a "retirement account" is a misnomer. Instead of thinking of your assets as "retirement savings" and "regular savings," you should instead think of them all as savings that are divided into "taxable" and "tax-deferred" portions.

The question of how these portions should be invested is a tax-planning decision that is determined after you have decided on the overall asset allocation of your total investment portfolio. Once you have decided on a given allocation, you should apportion the investments in such a way as to minimize taxes. If you are still working, most likely you are still adding to your savings, and that means you will be investing for tax efficiency as you go along.

When it comes to taxes, however, nothing is ever simple.

Any investment with high annual returns—whether they are from income, dividends or realized capital gains—benefits from deferring taxes, and the longer the deferral, the more those benefits are able to compound.

Taxes in tax-deferred accounts are deferred until the assets are withdrawn, at which time they are taxed as income at ordinary income tax rates. In the case of investments with capital gains, the advantage of the lower capital gains tax rate is lost if the asset is placed in a tax-deferred account. However, the advantages of deferring taxes are strong, and when allowed to compound over long time periods—15 to 20 years—they can overwhelm higher tax rates that must be paid on withdrawal for almost all investors other than those who will be in the highest income brackets (36% or above) during retirement.

The best of both worlds, of course, is an investment in which you can defer paying taxes, but which is then taxed at the capital gains rate. This can be accomplished if you hold individual stocks, since you have complete control of the timing decision as to when to sell and realize gains. Many individuals, though, do not hold onto individual stocks for time periods as long as 15 to 20 years.

Most stock mutual funds—even those that have very low portfolio turnover—produce at least some annual distributions. Studies indicate that even low distribution levels on an annual basis tend to tip the scales in favor of tax-deferred accounts for high-returning stock mutual funds.

As a rule of thumb, a tax-efficient portfolio is allocated as follows:

• The tax-deferred portion consists of higher-returning investments. Thus, if you hold both

Table 1.
Return Needed From Taxable Savings to Match
Aftertax Accumulation in a Tax-Deferred Plan*

Tax Rate (%)	Expected Return From Tax-Deferred Plan (%)		
	6.0%	8.0%	10.0%
15.0	7.1	9.4	11.8
28.0	8.3	11.1	13.9
31.0	8.7	11.6	14.5
36.0	9.4	12.5	15.6

* Assumes tax-deferred plan accumulations are not subject to 10% penalty for early withdrawal. Also assumes returns from taxable savings are taxed annually as income.

stock and bond mutual funds, the stock funds should be allocated to the tax-deferred portion since they tend to produce much higher average annual rates of return, even though bond funds tend to have larger annual distributions. If you hold several kinds of stock funds, those that tend to have higher average annual rates of return should be allocated to the tax-deferred portion—for instance, if you hold both aggressive growth and equity-income funds, the aggressive growth funds should be allocated to the tax-deferred portion, since they tend to produce higher annual returns.

- The taxable portion consists of lower-returning investments, such as balanced funds and bond funds; investments in which you have complete control over the timing decision and that you are likely to hold onto for long time periods, such as long-term individual stock holdings; and investments with built-in tax shelter advantages, such as municipal bonds.

Note that these descriptions of investment tax exposure don't mean you should include these investments in your portfolio—you may, for instance, have only low exposure investments in all of your savings portfolio.

There are two constraints that will limit your ability to structure a tax-efficient portfolio:

- The lack of liquidity of the tax-deferred portion, since money can't be easily withdrawn before age 59½ without penalty. For instance, money set aside for short-term emergencies should not be allocated to the tax-deferred portion, even though the likely investments (usually money market funds) have a higher tax exposure.

- The investment choices available for your tax-deferred portion. In particular, employer-sponsored retirement plans may have only a few selections. That means you may have to balance the advantages of a retirement plan (tax deferral and possible employer matches) against the advantages of an investment that might offer greater return potential. If your employer is making matching contributions, it is a no-brainer—you are clearly better off in the plan. If there are no matches, it is only a question of the tax trade-offs. A rough guide to the trade-off is provided in Table 1, which shows the return you would need to earn in a taxable savings account (assuming all earnings are taxed each year as income) to accumulate the same amount as the aftertax value of a tax-deferred plan with lower expected returns. If you can find an alternative that produces primarily long-term capital gains where taxes can be deferred, the necessary rate of return would be less than illustrated.

Your tuning will consist of balancing these tax considerations against the constraints.

Portfolio Maintenance
While no investor would consider it a drawback, successful investments can throw your portfolio out of whack by becoming so overweighted that your investment mix no longer reflects your original plan.

Table 2.
Tuning and Maintenance: An Example

Savings Portfolio

Holding	Category	Tax Status of Acc't	Beginning Am't Value as of 6/30/94	As a % of Tot	One-Yr. Ret. thru 6/30/95	Add t'ns	End Am't Value as of 6/30/95	As a % of Tot
Vanguard Index Trust–500	Large Cap	Tax-Deferred (401k)	$4,000	40%	25.8%	$2,310	$7,342	50%
Vanguard Int'l Value	Int'l	Tax-Deferred (401k)	1,500	15	2.1%	$690	2,221	15
Acorn	Small Cap	Tax-Deferred (IRA)*	1,000	10	13.3%	–	1,133	8
T. Rowe Price Eq Income	Large Cap	Tax-Deferred (IRA)*	1,000	10	21.7%	–	1,217	8
T. Rowe Price Interm. Treas.	Bond	Taxable	1,500	15	13.6%	–	1,704	12
Money Market Fund	Cash	Taxable	1,000	10	4.0%	–	1,040	7%
			$10,000	100%			$14,657	100%

*IRA Rollover

Asset Allocation

Asset Class	Beginning	Ending
Large-Cap Stocks	50%	58%
Small-Cap Stocks	10	8
International Stocks	15	15
Bonds	15	12
Cash	10	7
	100%	100%

During your working years, keeping your portfolio in balance with your original plan can be achieved in two ways:

- Through periodic additions to your savings, either on your own or through contributions to your employer-sponsored plans.

- By reallocating existing investments in your tax-deferred accounts where possible.

To keep your portfolio tuned, you should avoid incurring tax liabilities. For that reason, investments in your taxable portion should be sold only because of poor performance, not to rebalance your portfolio.

Which rebalancing approach is preferable?

Many individuals will be able to maintain their portfolio balance through proper allocation of their periodic contributions even when there are large variations in performance of the various parts. The larger your annual additions in relation to your beginning-of-the-year starting amount, the easier it will be to maintain balance through these periodic investments.

The ability to reallocate existing investments in tax-deferred accounts will depend on the limitations and number of alternatives available through your employee-sponsored plan. Assets in IRAs can be reallocated relatively easily if the IRA account offers various alternatives; otherwise, IRAs can be reallocated through trustee-to-trustee transfers, although this can be a hassle, and it must be done correctly to comply with all of the rules, since mistakes can be costly.

TUNING AND MAINTENANCE: AN EXAMPLE

An example of the process is illustrated in Table 2.

Last year, this investor started to look more closely at her savings portfolio. At the time, she had $10,000 in savings: $2,500 in taxable savings, $2,000 in an IRA (a rollover from a previous employer), and $5,500 accumulated and vested in her 401(k) plan. She also decided that, based on her circumstances and risk tolerance, she would like to allocate her savings portfolio as follows: 50% in large-cap stocks, 10% in small-cap stocks, 15% in international stocks (for an overall stock commitment of 75%), 15% in bonds, and 10% in cash.

Based on this commitment, the portfolio was allocated among taxable and tax-deferred accounts as tax efficiently as possible, given that her 401(k) plan only has four options—an index fund, an international fund, a bond fund, and a money market fund. Thus, she invested her 401(k) money in the highest-return areas, while she invested $1,500 of her taxable savings in the lower-return area. The IRA rollover was transferred to two new IRAs with higher returns—one invested in large-cap stocks, T. Rowe Price Equity Income Fund, and the other invested in small-cap stocks, Acorn Fund. And she kept 10% of her taxable savings invested in money market funds to provide liquidity for short-term emergencies.

To keep her portfolio in balance, she also had to determine how to allocate her periodic contributions for the upcoming year, which she determined would only be through contributions to her 401(k) plan, since she did not expect to be able to add to taxable savings.

How does she determine how much should go to each option?

To maintain balance, this investor allocates her retirement account contributions according to the percentages that they make up in her total portfolio. A small-cap investment is unavailable for her 401(k) contributions, and she prefers to keep the lower-returning bonds in her taxable accounts, so she must apportion according to the available investments: 50% to large-cap stocks and 15% to international. Together, these make up 65% of her total portfolio. Thus, 50% ÷ 65%, or 77%, should go to large-cap stocks, and 15% ÷ 65%, ·or 23%, should go to international. She informs her employer of these percentages, and her contributions are allocated accordingly.

How well was the balance maintained over the year?

You can see that the balance was fairly well maintained, even though the various parts performed quite differently over the time period. Why? Her contributions totaled $3,000, which is fairly large in relation to the $10,000 initial amount; these contributions have a greater impact on the percentage allocations than the additions (or losses) due to the investment performance of the funds.

At the end of the period, she is overly committed to large-cap stocks, and slightly undercommitted to bonds, small-cap stocks and cash—not surprising given the fact that she was unable to invest in either during the year. The commitment to international stocks held fairly steady.

Does anything need to be adjusted? She is only a few percentage points off from her bond and small-cap commitments, not enough to worry about at this stage. She should try to increase taxable savings and add to her cash reserves. She could also transfer some of the IRA rollover from the T. Rowe Price Equity Income Fund to the Acorn IRA to increase her small-cap investment, since she won't be able to make future contributions to this category from her salary deductions.

Keeping your investment program running smoothly involves periodic tuning and maintenance. Your goal is to stick to the investment plan and allocations you originally determined. Based on your original allocation decision, you should then:

- Keep your portfolio in tune by placing the allocations in the most tax-efficient part of your portfolio.

- Rebalance periodically to maintain the original allocations. You needn't aim for pinpoint accuracy, so don't worry about straying by a few percentage points.

If done on a regular basis, your costs in terms of time and money can be kept to a minimum.

10

Keeping Your Portfolio in Balance During Your Retirement Years

For high-wire artists, maintaining balance can be a matter of life or death.

Maintaining balance in your savings portfolio is not quite that critical, but it nonetheless is important to your financial well-being. It consists of rebalancing your portfolio to make sure that variations in performance of the individual items do not cause your overall asset allocation to stray too far from your original plan.

While all investors need to rebalance their portfolios periodically, the methods available differ depending on whether you are still working and continuing to save, or if you are in your retirement years, withdrawing money from savings on which to live.

The last chapter discussed rebalancing in your working years. This chapter focuses on retirement.

PORTFOLIO MAINTENANCE

During your retirement years, keeping your portfolio in balance with your original plan can be achieved in two ways:

- Through periodic withdrawals from your savings.

- By reallocating existing investments in your tax-deferred accounts where possible. Assets in IRAs can be reallocated through trustee-to-trustee transfers, although this can be a hassle and it must be done correctly to comply with all of the rules, since mistakes can be costly. Required distributions can complicate this, but your minimum distribution can come from any one (or combination) of your IRA accounts if they have the same beneficiaries (however, a minimum distribution amount must be determined for each account separately; your total minimum distribution is the sum of these individual IRA minimums).

To keep your portfolio in balance, you should avoid incurring tax liabilities. For that reason, investments in your taxable portion should be sold only because of poor performance or because you need the funds for income, not to rebalance your portfolio.

Invest for Returns, not Income

One of your goals will be to live off of your savings portfolio. That means that you will be withdrawing assets periodically.

How should these be withdrawn?

Some investors simply let the income payments or distributions determine how much to withdraw. The problem with this approach, however, is that it encourages you to meet income needs by putting savings in higher-yielding investments (such as bonds), which offer little opportunity for growth. The result is that over the long term, your savings—and the income it generates—is unable to grow enough to keep pace with inflation, and you may be faced with a lower standard of living.

It isn't necessary, however, to rely on this method of withdrawal. Instead, you can determine a "spending amount" to withdraw each year that is based, among other things, on your assumed rate of return on your savings [see "How Much of Your Savings Can You Afford to Spend During Retirement?" in the August 1995 AAII *Journal*]. The overall amount withdrawn can come from income payments, dividends, capital gains, or a combination. This approach encourages you to invest for total return, not simply income.

Many mutual funds offer withdrawal plans in which they automatically sell a specific dollar amount of shares, which is sent to you (or deposited in a money market fund) monthly, quarterly, semi-annually, or annually. Alternatively, you can determine for yourself which funds to withdraw from and sell shares accordingly.

Rebalancing Considerations

One problem that you will encounter is determining what is considered cash in your portfolio.

In your asset allocation plan, cash is considered a cushion to provide liquidity for emergencies, so that other more volatile assets do not need to be sold at possibly inopportune times. Your asset allocation plan also assumes a relatively steady allocation to cash.

Using this definition, your annual spending amounts should be excluded from your cash account when examining your asset allocation, even if the proceeds from distributions and sales are invested in your money market fund.

Why? First, at some point you will have spent all of your annual amount, and at that time, you should still have your desired cash commitment as a liquidity cushion. Second, as you spend money you will draw down your amount allocated to cash; if you were to determine your asset allocations at various points in the year and include the portion that you plan to spend, your asset allocations could vary by quite a bit.

The more practical approach is to simply take a snapshot picture of your portfolio at one point in time and exclude your annual spending amount from your total portfolio value and your cash position when determining your asset allocation.

Another consideration is your tax efficiency. You may or may not need to withdraw funds from your tax-deferred accounts, depending on your age (minimum distributions are required after age 70½).

If you are required to take distributions from your IRAs, it may be more difficult to rebalance using simply your withdrawal amounts. One option would be to transfer your IRA to a mutual fund family with numerous fund options; rebalancing could then be accomplished by simply moving assets among the various categories.

REBALANCING: AN EXAMPLE

An example of the process is illustrated in Table 1.

At the end of last year, Peter Olsen retired. Six months prior to his retirement, he had accumulated a total savings portfolio of $300,000, with $75,000 in IRA accounts, and $225,000 in taxable savings. These savings are needed to supplement the pension and Social Security annual payments Mr. Olsen will receive, and he expects that he will need to withdraw roughly $21,000 a year. Mr. Olsen implemented his plan six months prior to retirement so that he could reassess his position six months after retirement using one year's worth of performance data.

Several years prior to retirement, Mr. Olsen assessed his circumstances and decided on a desired asset allocation consisting of a 50% commitment to equities (30% to large-cap stocks, 10% to small-cap stocks, and 10% to international stocks), 40% in bonds, and 10% in a money market fund to provide liquidity for emergencies and to temper the volatility of the portfolio's value. Based on this desired commitment, he gradually changed the composition of his savings portfolio to reflect his desired allocation, as well as his "spending" (withdrawal) needs. By the middle of last year, just prior to retirement, his savings portfolio reflected this new allocation goal: an S&P 500 index fund and an equity-income fund represented his large-cap commitment, his small-cap commitment was invested in a low turnover aggressive growth fund, his international and bond commitments were both in mutual funds, and his cash commitment was in a money market fund (see Table 1).

Because he is still some years away from age 70½, Mr. Olsen does not need to withdraw from his IRAs immediately. In terms of tax efficiency, he should allocate his highest-returning investments to this tax-deferred portion of his portfolio. He decided to put a bond fund, a low turnover S&P 500 index fund, and an international fund in his taxable accounts and use distributions as part of his annual spending amount. He put the remainder of his large-cap commitment as well as his aggressive growth fund (which invests in small-cap stocks) in an IRA.

During the following year, the funds turned in varied performances, as indicated in Table 1. Mr. Olsen also received distributions from his S&P 500 fund, his international fund, and his interme-

Table 1.
Portfolio Rebalancing During Retirement: An Example

Savings Portfolio

Holding	Type of Account	Beginning Amount Value as of 6/30/94 ($)	As a % of Total (%)	Return thru 6/30/95 (%)	Distributions (to MMF) ($)	Value as of 6/30/95 ($)	Action	Value After Sale ($)
Equity-Income Fund	IRA	45,000	15	25.8	Reinvested	56,610	Sell $9,302	47,308
S&P 500 Index Fund	Taxable	45,000	15	21.7	2,409	52,356	None	52,356
Aggressive Grth Fund	IRA	30,000	10	13.3	Reinvested	33,990	None	33,990
International Fund	Taxable	30,000	10	22.4	2,358	34,362	None	34,362
Inter-Term Bond Fund	Taxable	120,000	40	13.6	8,861	127,459	None	127,459
Money Market Fund	Taxable	30,000	10	3.0	Reinvested	44,528	None	53,830
	Total:	$300,000	100%			Total: $349,305		Total: $349,305
					Tot Ex Spend Amt:	$328,305	Tot Ex Spend Amt:	$328,305

Asset Allocation

Asset Class	Desired (%)	6/30/95 Total (%)	6/30/95 Ex Spend Amt* (%)	After Sale Total (%)	After Sale Ex Spend Amt* (%)
Large Cap Stocks:	30	31.2	33.2	28.5	30.4
Small Cap Stocks:	10	9.7	10.3	9.7	10.3
International Stocks:	10	9.8	10.5	9.8	10.5
Bonds:	40	36.5	38.8	36.5	38.8
Cash:	10	12.8	7.2	15.4	10.0

* Ex Spend Amt: Value After Sale ÷ Total Ex Spend Amount. Spending amount is also excluded from value of money market fund for cash portion.

diate-term bond fund, which he has automatically distributed to his money market fund. Thus, the values of the various funds at the end of the year reflect not only performance, but the distribution pattern Mr. Olsen has chosen.

The distributions Mr. Olsen put into his money market fund are less than the $21,000 he needs annually. That means he needs to sell some shares to make up the difference.

Which funds should he withdraw from to keep the portfolio in balance?

The second part of Table 1 indicates Mr. Olsen's desired asset allocation, as well as his actual asset allocation at the end of the time period. The column labeled "Ex Spend Amt" indicates the end-period asset allocation, excluding the $21,000 that will ultimately be withdrawn and "spent" from the total portfolio value and the money market fund. The figures indicate that Mr. Olsen's large-cap commitment is the most overcommitted. In addition, his cash commitment is very low. If he were to maintain his "desired" allocation, his money market fund should have $32,830 after he spends his $21,000 (10% of $328,305); thus, he can only spend $11,698 from his current money market fund balance ($44,528 – $32,830). That, in turn, means that ideally he should sell more shares than he originally thought—$9,302 ($21,000 – $11,698)—rather than his total distributions to maintain his liquidity.

Since he is overcommitted to large-cap stocks, Mr. Olsen also decides to sell shares from his S&P 500 index fund.

How does the allocation look after the sale? Table 1 indicates that, excluding the $21,000 he will ultimately withdraw, he is within several percentage points of his desired allocation—close enough to maintain peace of mind. In all likelihood, the bond portion will continue to fall behind, since there is no growth component. At that time, Mr. Olsen may want to add to his bond commitment by shifting assets in his IRA accounts to a bond fund.

Keeping your investment program running smoothly involves periodic rebalancing, even in retirement. Your goal is to stick to the investment plan and allocations you originally determined. Here are some points to keep in mind:

- Distributing funds between your taxable accounts and tax-deferred accounts is a judgment call. In general, you should putt your higher-returning assets in the tax-deferred portion. However, you may need to have a small bond portion in your tax-deferred accounts to help keep your balance, since you will be withdrawing from your taxable accounts, and there is little growth to fixed-income funds.

- Keep your portfolio balanced by withdrawing from assets in which you are overcommitted, and by shifting assets in tax-deferred accounts.

- Rebalancing does not need to be frequent—semiannually or annually should be sufficient. However, your actual portfolio allocations will be constantly changing due to varying performances and particularly as you withdraw spending funds. Use a snapshot picture of your portfolio that excludes your spending amount to rebalance.

- Don't worry about straying from your desired allocation by a few percentage points. Aim for a general target, not pinpoint accuracy.